# MEN ALSO CRY

For information, contact:
Divyam Agarwal
contact@divyamagarwal.com

Cover design by Divyam Agarwal
Printed in India

ISBN: 978-93-342-1195-5

**Disclaimer:**
The views and opinions expressed in this book are those of the author and do not necessarily reflect the views of the publisher or any affiliated organization.

A man walks with the world on his shoulders,
His pain hidden in the corners of his smile,
Where words fail, and silence screams louder,
No one notices, no one cares.
Men also cry.

In the dark of night, when the world sleeps,
He sheds tears that no one sees,
In his own solitude, his heart breaks,
A silent warrior, fighting his fears.
Men also cry.

The world expects him to never fall,
But who holds him when he hits the wall?
The weight of expectations makes him small,
Still, he stands tall.
Men also cry.

He hides the words that burn within,
Carrying them in his heart, a heavy sin,
Afraid that if he speaks, he'll break,
He'll lose the respect, for his own sake.
Men also cry.

No medals for the wars he fights,
No applause for the sleepless nights,
A man's battle is often unseen,
Fought in silence, between the screams.
Men also cry.

# The Face He Wears

In a world where men are told to be tough,
To carry the weight of the world without a puff,
He wears a mask, polished and strong,
Hiding his true self all along.

Beneath the tough exterior, there's a soft heart,
A soul that feels, yet keeps its part,
In a game of survival, he learns to suppress,
Emotions buried deep in the depths of distress.

His face tells a story of strength and pride,
But it's just a façade he's forced to hide,
The tears he's shed, the pain he's known,
Are buried deep, where no one's shown.

They say men don't cry, that's not their way,
But the weight of the world makes him break every day.
When no one's watching, when no one's near,
He lets out the pain, letting go of the fear.

Yet when the world looks, he stands so tall,
A fortress of strength, unyielding to all.
But who will hold him when he falls apart?
Who will listen to the cries of his heart?

He fights to be the man they expect him to be,
But deep inside, he longs to be free.

Free from the weight, the stress, the shame,
To let go, to show that he's just the same.

**Men also cry.**
But who will see?

# Unspoken Words

He speaks in silence,
His words trapped within,
Afraid to voice the pain,
That echoes deep inside his skin.

He was taught to be strong,
To never let his guard down,
But the weight of unspoken words,
Has him drowning, slowly, to drown.

There are thoughts that swirl,
Wounds that fester and burn,
But his lips remain sealed tight,
For fear that the world might turn.

No one asks him what he feels,
No one dares to understand,
So he wears the quiet mask,
And holds it in with trembling hands.

The sadness in his eyes is clear,
But he knows he can't show his fear,
To speak would make him seem weak,
So he swallows the words, too afraid to speak.

He carries the weight of regrets,
The "what ifs" and the unsaid bets,

But who will listen, who will care?
When he's too busy hiding his despair.

What if he could open up,
Let his heart speak without the block?
What if the world would hear him out,
And see the pain behind the doubt?

But for now, he stays silent,
A storm brewing deep inside,
Unspoken words, untold stories,
A man's heart, where his tears reside.

**Men also cry.**
But who will listen?

# The Illusion of Strength

Every day, he puts on a smile,
Hiding the pain he's carried for miles,
A mask of strength, a shield so strong,
That no one knows where he truly belongs.

He's the protector, the provider, the one,
The one who never lets the job be undone,
But in his chest, his heart pounds with fear,
That no one will see the man breaking here.

The world expects him to always be tough,
But sometimes the road gets too rough.
Yet he'll never show it, never admit,
That the burden's too much for him to fit.

The weight of his family, the weight of his dreams,
The silent pressure that rips at the seams,
He grits his teeth and bears it all,
But behind the mask, he begins to fall.

He's afraid to admit that he's not okay,
That some nights he just wants to slip away,
But the world would never understand,
So he stands tall, with no helping hand.

He's taught to be the rock, never the stream,
The man who's invincible, the one who beams,

But in the quiet moments, when no one's around,
He collapses inward, with no sound.

His tears are silent, his sobs unheard,
A man of strength, but so deeply stirred,
Will anyone ever see the cracks in his mask,
Or is he doomed to hide behind the task?

**Men also cry.**
But no one sees the cracks.

# A Heart That Breaks in Silence

No one hears the silent cry,
The plea for help that fades, gone by,
A man's heart breaks quietly,
As the world keeps moving, endlessly.

The weight of his love, the weight of his care,
He holds it all in, pretending it's fair,
For the world expects him to stay strong,
To carry the burdens, to just move along.

But inside, his heart is torn apart,
A thousand pieces of shattered art,
He loves so deeply, yet feels so alone,
Afraid to admit the cracks that have grown.

He hides his pain behind a smile,
Takes a deep breath, and stays for a while,
But every step he takes, every word he says,
Is a mask to cover the hurt that never decays.

When the night falls, and no one's there,
He lets his heart break, with no one to care,
The tears fall quietly, with no one to see,
A man's heart breaking in a world that's busy.

His love for others, his care for the world,
Makes him feel like he should be unfurled,

But who will care when he's the one who breaks?
Who will hold him when his heart aches?

He carries on, as if nothing's wrong,
But inside, he's struggling to belong,
For even men with hearts so strong,
Need someone to help them carry on.

**Men also cry.**
But no one hears.

# When the World Turns its Back

He's always there for everyone,
The one you call when the day's undone,
The one who listens, the one who cares,
But who's there for him when life's unfair?

He gives his all, without a thought,
Hoping that the love he gives is caught,
Yet when he needs it, when he's down,
The world's too busy to turn around.

He's taught to stand tall and never complain,
To shoulder the burden, to bear the pain,
But in the quiet moments, when no one's near,
He feels the sting of loneliness, clear.

When the world turns its back on him,
He wonders why the lights are dim,
He gave so much, he fought so hard,
But still, he's left with a broken shard.

The people he cared for, the ones he loved,
Seem to vanish when push comes to shove,
Leaving him alone in the darkest night,
Wondering why he keeps up the fight.

He's expected to be the strong, steady hand,
But when he falls, who will understand?

He wears his pain as a badge of pride,
But inside, he's dying, trying to hide.

Why does he give, and yet receive so little?
Why does the world seem to always belittle?
In a sea of faces, he's lost in the crowd,
His cries unheard, his voice not allowed.

**Men also cry.**
But no one is there.

# Fear of Being Weak

He walks with the weight of the world,
Afraid that if he falters, he'll be unfurled,
That the walls he's built will all come down,
And the world will see the cracks, the frown.

To admit he's scared, to say he's lost,
Would cost him everything he's tried to emboss,
A man who never shows his fear,
But inside, the storm is crystal clear.

He's told to be fearless, to never be small,
To keep going, no matter how hard the fall,
But the pressure builds, day by day,
And inside, his strength starts to decay.

What if he's not enough?
What if the burden's too rough?
What if the world sees the cracks in his pride?
What if he no longer has the strength to hide?

The fear of weakness, the fear of shame,
The fear that his struggles will tarnish his name,
So he stays silent, with his head held high,
Not letting anyone see him cry.

But in the dead of night, when no one's near,
He lets himself go, shedding the fear,

For a moment, he's not the strong, brave man,
He's just a human, doing the best he can.

The fear of being weak is a heavy chain,
That locks him inside, again and again,
But sometimes, even the strongest need to fall,
To show the world that it's okay to call.

**Men also cry.**
But they're afraid to be weak.

# Carrying the Weight of Others

He's the one people turn to,
The rock, the constant, the glue,
Everyone leans on him for strength,
He carries it all, no matter the length.

He picks up the pieces of broken dreams,
Puts them together with silent schemes,
He shoulders the weight, without a word,
Yet when he's broken, it goes unheard.

The world expects him to be the guide,
The one who keeps the storms outside,
He bears the pain, the guilt, the sorrow,
Fearing he might not make it to tomorrow.

But who carries his weight? Who feels his strain?
Who listens when he says he's in pain?
He's too busy helping, too busy giving,
Too busy making sure others are living.

When does he get the chance to breathe?
When can he let go, to finally grieve?
The world doesn't stop, it never slows,
And he keeps running, nobody knows.

He dreams of a moment to just be still,
To drop the load, to heal, to rebuild,

But he continues to carry the weight of the world,
A man who's exhausted, yet never unfurled.

His heart aches with the burden of love,
Of caring for others, pushing beyond,
But who will care when he's fallen apart?
Who will notice the cracks in his heart?

**Men also cry.**
But they carry the world alone.

# The Unacknowledged Hero

He walks unnoticed through crowded streets,
His sacrifices hidden beneath the feats,
The quiet hero with no applause,
Fighting battles with no applause.

He doesn't wear a cape or shine in the light,
His victories are quiet, out of sight,
Yet he gives all he has, every single day,
Without a word, without any display.

No one thanks him for the work he does,
No one notices the silent fuss,
The hours he puts in, the sweat and strain,
The pain that's hidden, his inner chain.

He's the unsung hero, the man behind,
The one who fights, who's left behind,
The one who keeps things together, tight,
While he's dying quietly, out of sight.

His sacrifices go unnoticed by most,
But he keeps going, doing what he's supposed,
Because that's what he's been taught to be,
The silent worker, the one who's free.

But when does he get his due?
When will someone see the struggle he's been through?

The quiet battles, the tears he's shed,
The times he wanted to give up, but instead...

He keeps going, because he's a man,
Doing what needs to be done, without a plan,
Fighting battles no one will see,
But deep inside, he yearns to be free.

**Men also cry.**
But they're the unacknowledged heroes.

# Lonely in a Crowd

Surrounded by faces, but he feels alone,
In a room full of people, he's on his own,
The laughter echoes, the voices ring,
But his heart is quiet, not a thing.

He watches the world go on with ease,
Everyone connected, everyone at peace,
But he stands apart, on the outside,
Hiding the storm that's brewing inside.

The weight of loneliness is hard to bear,
When you're surrounded, yet no one's there,
They see him, but they don't really know,
The pain he carries, the tears he's let go.

He smiles and laughs with the crowd,
But inside, his heart is screaming loud,
He wonders if anyone will ever see,
The man he is, the pain he carries silently.

In the crowd, he's just another face,
No one notices his desperate chase,
To find someone who will understand,
Someone who will hold his trembling hand.

But he keeps his distance, keeps it inside,
Afraid to show the hurt he tries to hide,

For what if they laugh? What if they leave?
What if they can't help, or choose not to believe?

He longs for connection, for someone to care,
For someone to notice the burden he bears,
But for now, he stands in the crowd, unseen,
A man who's lonely, caught in between.

**Men also cry.**
But they're lonely in a crowd.

# The Quiet Cry

In the stillness of the night, when the world is asleep,
He lets his heart ache, and his thoughts begin to creep,
The tears fall softly, without a sound,
A quiet cry, when no one's around.

He's never been taught that it's okay to break,
That it's okay to cry, to make mistakes,
So he hides his emotions, bottles them in,
Afraid of the judgment, afraid of the sin.

He cries in silence, his soul heavy with grief,
Hoping for solace, for some kind of relief,
But the world doesn't hear, the world doesn't see,
The man behind the mask, longing to be free.

His pain is quiet, his grief is deep,
But he knows he must carry it, never to weep,
For a man who cries is seen as weak,
And that's a fear he'll never speak.

Yet inside, his heart is torn apart,
A battlefield, where emotions start,
To clash and collide, in a storm so strong,
But still, he holds on, pretending he belongs.

The quiet cry is a man's silent plea,
A call for help that no one can see,

He cries alone, in the silence of night,
Afraid to show that he's not alright.

But sometimes, even the strongest must fall,
They must face the truth and stand tall,
For a man's heart is not made of stone,
And sometimes, he just needs to be shown.

**Men also cry.**
But they cry quietly, alone.

# The Burden of Expectations

He wakes each day with a heavy heart,
Carrying the weight of expectations from the start,
The world tells him who he must be,
But inside, he longs to just be free.

A man of strength, a man of might,
The one who's always ready to fight,
He's told to provide, to never falter,
To be the rock, the one they can alter.

The pressure is constant, the burden too much,
To meet every standard, to never lose touch,
To be the perfect son, the perfect friend,
The one who never breaks, who can always transcend.

But deep inside, he wonders why,
Why he's asked to always comply,
Why he's never allowed to feel,
Why his own needs are never real.

Every day, he wears the mask of pride,
Hiding the hurt he keeps inside,
He's expected to smile, to always succeed,
While silently, his soul begins to bleed.

He wonders if anyone will ever see,
The cracks in his armor, the truth in his plea,

To be accepted for who he is, not what he's told,
To be loved for his heart, and not for his role.

But the world keeps pushing, keeps demanding more,
And he keeps giving, hoping it's not a bore,
But he's tired, so tired, of pretending to be,
The man the world wants him to be.

**Men also cry.**
But they are burdened by expectations.

# The Anxiety of Losing Control

He holds his emotions with a firm grip,
Afraid that one slip will make him slip,
A tiny crack, a single tear,
And all his strength will disappear.

He's taught to control, to never let go,
To keep it together, to put on a show,
For if he loses control, if he breaks down,
He fears he'll fall, and no one will be around.

The fear of weakness, the fear of collapse,
Keeps him bound in invisible traps,
Every moment, every breath,
He battles with the fear of emotional death.

What if he can't handle the pain?
What if his heart breaks once again?
What if he can't find his way,
And everything he's built starts to decay?

He fights with every ounce of his will,
To keep his emotions under control, still,
But in the quiet corners of his mind,
The fear of losing himself is all he can find.

He wonders if anyone would understand,
If he fell apart and showed his hand,

Would they still see him as strong and true,
Or would they turn away, like they always do?

He holds on, tighter each day,
Afraid that if he lets go, he'll fade away,
But the weight of his fear, the burden of the fight,
Makes every day feel like a desperate night.

**Men also cry.**
But they're afraid to lose control.

# The Forgotten Self

In the chaos of life, he fades away,
Losing sight of who he is each day,
He gives so much, but forgets to ask,
What does he need behind the mask?

He's always there for those he loves,
But who's there for him, when push comes to shove?
The man who sacrifices, who gives his all,
But in the end, he's the one who falls.

His dreams are set aside, his hopes deferred,
For the ones he loves, for the ones who've heard,
But in the quiet moments, when he's alone,
He wonders if anyone knows the man he's grown.

His identity fades with each passing year,
A shadow of the man he once held dear,
He's lost in the roles he's forced to play,
And the person he was, has drifted away.

He gave up his dreams for others' sake,
But now, he's wondering what it would take,
To remember who he was, before the fight,
To rediscover the man who was once so bright.

But the world demands more than he can give,
And the man he was no longer lives,

He's become a part of everyone else's plan,
A forgotten soul, lost in the sand.

He longs for a moment, a chance to be,
The man he once was, wild and free,
But the forgotten self is hard to find,
Buried beneath the weight of a busy mind.

**Men also cry.**
But they've forgotten who they are.

# The Burden of Being Strong

He's always the one who holds the line,
The pillar of strength, the steady sign,
When others fall, he stands tall,
But who will catch him when he starts to fall?

He's the rock, the unwavering base,
The one who always keeps up the pace,
But inside, the weight is wearing him thin,
A burden so heavy, it's hard to begin.

He's taught that strength is never in tears,
That real men don't show their fears,
But every day, he carries the load,
Afraid to crack, afraid to explode.

The burden of strength is an endless fight,
To keep it together, to be the light,
But what happens when the light starts to fade?
When the strength he has begins to degrade?

He pushes through, he wears the mask,
Pretending everything is under task,
But inside, the cracks begin to show,
As the weight of life starts to grow.

He wonders if he'll ever get the chance,
To rest, to breathe, to let go of the dance,

Of always being strong, always being right,
When sometimes, he just wants to fight.

To fight for the right to feel the pain,
To fight for the right to break the chain,
To be weak, to be vulnerable, to fall,
And to finally admit that he's not strong at all.

**Men also cry.**
But they carry the burden of being strong.

# Behind the Mask

Every day, he wears a mask,
A smile, a persona, the perfect task,
He hides his pain, his fears, his flaws,
Behind the mask, he's free from pause.

The world sees him as perfect and whole,
A man with purpose, a man with a goal,
But behind those eyes, behind the gaze,
Is a soul lost in a labyrinth, a never-ending maze.

He's told to be strong, to never let down,
To wear the mask, and never frown,
But every night, when the world sleeps tight,
He wonders if he'll ever be alright.

The mask he wears is made of pride,
A shield to hide what's deep inside,
The loneliness, the pain, the strife,
The side of him that struggles with life.

He wishes someone could see through,
The mask he wears, the life he's glued,
But how could they know, when he's never shown,
The man who's hidden, all on his own?

He's tired of pretending, of putting on a show,
Of being the strong one, never letting go,

But he's afraid of what will happen if he breaks,
Afraid of the consequences, the heartache it takes.

So behind the mask, he stays confined,
Afraid of being seen, afraid to find,
That the world won't accept him if he's real,
That no one will care, or know how to feel.

**Men also cry.**
But they hide behind the mask.

# The Silent Battle

Every day, he fights a battle no one can see,
A war inside, where he's never truly free,
The scars are hidden, the wounds don't show,
But inside, the pain continues to grow.

He faces the world with a stoic face,
Not allowing anyone to see the trace,
Of the struggles he's fought, the tears he's cried,
The moments he's felt lost, the times he's died.

The battle rages, and he's on his own,
Fighting a war in silence, unknown,
He keeps moving forward, day by day,
Hoping somehow, he'll find his way.

The pressure builds, the weight too much,
The expectation, the constant touch,
Of the world telling him he must succeed,
Ignoring the fact that he's in need.

He battles through the pain, through the strain,
Hiding the loss, hiding the gain,
For fear that if he shows what's real,
He'll be seen as weak, unable to heal.

But the silent battle is taking its toll,
It's slowly breaking him, body and soul,

And yet, he keeps going, keeps pushing through,
Even though he doesn't know what to do.

Sometimes he wonders how much more he can take,
Before the silence becomes too much to fake,
Before the battle finally breaks him down,
And the mask he wears starts to drown.

**Men also cry.**
But they fight a silent battle.

# The Pressure of Expectations

He wakes each morning with a heavy heart,
The world demands more, it won't let him depart,
From the roles he must play, the man he must be,
The expectations suffocating him, making him feel small, yet free.

He's told to be strong, to lead the way,
To never give up, to never sway,
But each day feels like a mountain too tall,
With no one to help, no one to call.

The weight of success, the need to achieve,
To be perfect, to never deceive,
It all falls on his shoulders, a constant strain,
A pressure that grows with every gain.

He wonders if anyone will ever see,
The cost of perfection, the toll it takes to be,
The man who never falters, the man who's bold,
When inside, he's broken, and feeling cold.

He's the one everyone looks up to,
The one who always knows what to do,
But when does he get to break, to fall,
And not be judged, not be dismissed at all?

The burden of expectations is heavy, indeed,
It chokes his spirit, feeds his greed,

For success is always just out of reach,
And he's too tired to continue the speech.

He longs for a moment to just be him,
To drop the mask, to stop pretending on a whim,
But the world won't let him, the world won't care,
For the man who's strong, but always there.

**Men also cry.**
But they bear the pressure of expectations.

# The Quiet Strength

He doesn't raise his voice, doesn't make a scene,
Yet his strength is evident, strong and serene,
He carries the world on his tired shoulders,
With a quiet strength, as he grows older.

He doesn't need to prove himself loud,
Doesn’t seek praise, doesn’t stand proud,
But his actions speak louder than words ever could,
His silence, a testament to doing good.

He’s the man who stands in the shadows, unseen,
Yet he’s the one holding everything between,
The one who picks up the pieces, the one who stays,
The one who endures, through the toughest days.

His strength isn’t shown in muscles or might,
It’s in the moments he chooses to fight,
When the world is against him, when it’s all too much,
He stands still, silently, his heart as such.

The quiet strength of a man who endures,
Who never shows weakness, who never implores,
Who holds his tears back, hides his grief,
While silently, he’s searching for relief.

He doesn’t need to say a word, doesn’t need to show,
He keeps moving forward, letting his heart glow,

For in his quiet strength lies the truth,
That real power comes from bearing the proof.

But even the strongest need rest, need care,
Even the quiet need someone there,
To see through the silence, to notice the strain,
To help him heal, to ease the pain.

**Men also cry.**
But their strength is quiet.

# The Weight of Unspoken Words

He holds so much inside, but says so little,
The thoughts, the feelings, the pain so brittle,
He never speaks of the struggles he faces,
The inner battles, the silent embraces.

Every word he doesn't say is a weight on his chest,
A burden he carries, a wound that won't rest,
He wishes someone would hear the cries in his mind,
But the words stay locked, too afraid to unwind.

He's taught to be strong, to never complain,
To keep it inside, to endure the pain,
But in the silence, his heart starts to break,
As every unspoken word is too much to take.

He wonders if anyone would ever see,
The depth of his silence, the plea to be free,
The words left unsaid, the feelings ignored,
The cries for help, forever stored.

He longs for a moment to let it all out,
To speak his truth, to let go of doubt,
But the fear of judgment holds him back,
The fear of being seen as broken, a lack.

The weight of unspoken words is a heavy load,
A burden that follows him down the road,

And yet, he smiles, he keeps moving along,
While the unspoken words continue to prolong.

But every man has his breaking point,
Every heart has a moment to anoint,
The silence will crack, the words will flow,
And in that moment, the man will know.

**Men also cry.**
But their tears are made of unspoken words.

# The Struggle for Acceptance

He stands in the crowd, a face in the mass,
Hoping for a glance, hoping it'll pass,
The yearning for acceptance, a deep, quiet plea,
To be seen for who he is, not what he's meant to be.

He hides his vulnerability, fearing rejection,
The fear of not being enough, not gaining affection,
Always striving to be something more,
But still, he's left wanting, feeling unsure.

He's told to be tough, to never show need,
To keep pushing forward, to always succeed,
But inside, the hunger for love never fades,
For the approval of others, the validation he craves.

He wonders if anyone sees past the front,
If they know the man beneath, the one who confronts,
The insecurities, the flaws, the scars,
The heart that aches under the weight of the stars.

He strives to belong, to find his place,
But in the search, he's lost in space,
The constant battle to fit the mold,
To be someone he's not, to fit the role he's sold.

Yet the real man, the one deep inside,
Longs to be free, to no longer hide,

To be accepted as he is, without fear,
To find a place where he's truly near.

But the world judges, the world decides,
What's worthy, what's true, who gets to abide,
In the circle of acceptance, the world of grace,
Leaving him wondering if he has a place.

**Men also cry.**
But they long for acceptance.

# The Price of Sacrifice

He gives without measure, without complaint,
A silent hero, a selfless saint,
Always putting others before his own,
Yet in his giving, he feels alone.

The dreams he had, the life he envisioned,
Set aside for someone else's mission,
He sacrifices his wants, his time, his need,
To nurture others, to help them succeed.

But in the quiet of the night, he wonders why,
Why his sacrifices go unseen, as time passes by,
He doesn't ask for much, just a simple glance,
A token of gratitude, a chance for romance.

He works in the shadows, unnoticed, unseen,
His love is silent, but it's pure and clean,
Yet the cost of giving all that he can,
Leaves him feeling less than a man.

He misses the days when he lived for himself,
Before his dreams were stored on a dusty shelf,
But the love he feels for those he serves,
Keeps him going, though he gets less than he deserves.

The cost of sacrifice is more than they see,
It's a part of his soul, his identity,

He wonders if one day they'll understand,
The weight of giving all at his own hand.

He doesn't need riches, he doesn't need fame,
He just wants someone to call his name,
To see his sacrifices, to hold him near,
To tell him his worth, to make it clear.

**Men also cry.**
But they pay the price of sacrifice.

# The Fragility of Strength

The world calls him strong, unshaken, and bold,
A man who endures, whose story's untold,
But beneath the surface, where no one can see,
Lies a fragile heart yearning to be free.

Strength, they say, is to never fall,
To never waver, to stand tall,
But what of the days when his spirit bends,
When he feels like a flame the wind intends to end?

The cracks in his armor, invisible to sight,
Are scars of battles fought in the quiet night,
He pieces himself together, again and again,
Hiding the moments he's been broken within.

They see his resilience, his unyielding face,
But ignore the fragility he tries to erase,
He's human too, with fears and dreams,
A soul that's not as indestructible as it seems.

Strength is not in the absence of tears,
It's in carrying on despite the fears,
It's in admitting when the weight is too much,
In allowing himself to feel human's touch.

But he doesn't show it; he hides it away,
Afraid that his vulnerability might betray,

The image of strength the world holds dear,
A man unshaken, with no room for fear.

Yet, in his quiet moments, he knows,
True strength is found when fragility shows,
When he allows himself to feel, to break,
To let others in, for his own sake.

**Men also cry.**
For even strength can be fragile.

# The Unseen Apologies

He carries apologies he'll never voice,
For the times he stumbled, for every wrong choice,
Not because he's unwilling, not because of pride,
But because he's afraid they'll be pushed aside.

He apologizes in silence, with actions and care,
Through the things he fixes, through just being there,
Hoping his gestures speak louder than words,
Yet his heart aches for those apologies unheard.

He regrets the moments he fell short,
The dreams he couldn't build, the battles he fought,
But no one sees the guilt in his eyes,
No one hears the whispers of his quiet cries.

For every time he lost his way,
For every promise he couldn't repay,
He carries the weight of those he let down,
Hiding his guilt beneath a stoic frown.

He wants to say, "I'm sorry" out loud,
To lift the burden that's shrouded by the crowd,
But fear grips him, holding him still,
What if they don't forgive, what if they never will?

So, he buries the words deep in his chest,
Trying his hardest, giving his best,

To make amends through deeds, not speech,
Hoping his efforts will someday reach.

But the truth remains, unspoken, unfree,
Apologies locked where no one can see,
And though he may never say the words outright,
They linger in his heart every day, every night.

**Men also cry.**
For the apologies they never speak.

# The Love He Doesn't Show

He loves in ways that often go unseen,
Not through grand gestures or moments serene,
But in the quiet, the small things he does,
In his silent presence, in his unsaid trust.

He doesn't always say the words out loud,
But his actions speak volumes, quiet yet proud,
From fixing what's broken to staying up late,
Ensuring comfort, sealing every fate.

He shows love in sacrifices, big and small,
In carrying burdens so others don't fall,
In working hard without a complaint,
Even when his strength feels faint.

His love isn't flashy, it doesn't shout,
It's in his steadiness, removing doubt,
It's in the way he remembers the little things,
The songs you hum, the joy it brings.

He hides his tenderness behind a tough guise,
Fearing it'll be mistaken, dismissed, or despised,
For the world tells him men must be strong,
That showing affection is where they don't belong.

But if you look closer, beyond the shield,
You'll see a heart that's soft, unsealed,

A love so deep, it's hard to convey,
Yet it's there in everything, every day.

He loves with a strength that's quiet and true,
Through storms and trials, he'll see it through,
Even if he never speaks what he feels,
His love is evident in the life he builds.

**Men also cry.**
For the love they cannot show.

# The Fear of Failure

Failure looms like a shadow in his mind,
A constant reminder, unyielding, unkind,
He's told to succeed, to lead, to provide,
But what if he stumbles? What if he's tried?

The fear of falling, of losing it all,
Of not standing tall when the world makes a call,
It eats at his peace, it gnaws at his soul,
The pressure to perform takes a heavy toll.

He fears the disappointment in their eyes,
The unspoken judgment, the quiet sighs,
He's afraid of letting them down, of not being enough,
Of proving that even the strong have it tough.

The weight of expectations sits on his chest,
A relentless force, denying him rest,
He works harder, he pushes beyond,
Hoping to build what they'll depend on.

But what happens when he meets defeat?
When his plans unravel, when dreams retreat?
Who will catch him, who will say,
"It's okay to fail, it's okay to stray"?

The truth he hides, the fear he won't share,
Is that even in failure, he needs someone there,

To remind him he's human, that it's part of the fight,
That even in darkness, he still holds light.

For failure doesn't define the man within,
It's the courage to rise that begins again,
And though he may falter, his heart remains true,
A warrior at heart, breaking through.

**Men also cry.**
For the fear of failure they bury inside.

# The Invisible Grief

He grieves in silence, without a tear,
For the losses he's faced, for the ones held dear,
The world expects him to carry on,
To shoulder the pain until it's gone.

But grief doesn't vanish; it doesn't fade,
It lingers in the heart, in the promises made,
The loved ones lost, the dreams that died,
He mourns them alone, with no one by his side.

There's no room for his sorrow in a world so fast,
Where men are taught to bury the past,
To move forward, to leave it behind,
To hide the ache that echoes in his mind.

He's expected to be the pillar, the stone,
But even the strongest can feel alone,
For in his grief, there's no outlet, no voice,
No space to cry, no comforting choice.

He remembers the moments, the laughter, the love,
The bonds unbroken, now stars above,
But the weight of the loss is too much to bear,
And yet, he tells no one; he doesn't dare.

The invisible grief becomes part of his soul,
A shadow he carries, never whole,

Yet in his silence, he still finds a way,
To honor the memories and face each day.

For grief doesn't mean weakness; it's proof of the heart,
A testament to love that refuses to part,
And though the world may not see his pain,
It lives within him, again and again.

**Men also cry.**
For the grief they carry in silence.

# The Battle with Loneliness

He sits in a room filled with noise and life,
Yet feels the sting of a quiet knife,
For even surrounded, he feels unseen,
A lone figure in a crowded scene.

Loneliness isn't just the absence of a crowd,
It's the lack of connection, the silence so loud,
It's not being understood, not being known,
It's standing in company but feeling alone.

He builds walls to protect, to guard his heart,
But those same walls keep others apart,
He yearns for someone to break through the shield,
To understand the wounds he's yet to reveal.

Society tells him to be strong, self-contained,
To suppress his emotions, to keep them restrained,
But in his solitude, the weight starts to grow,
A quiet ache that few will know.

He longs for a voice, a hand to hold,
A connection so warm, breaking the cold,
Someone who sees him, beyond the façade,
Who knows his fears and the battles he's fought.

But he struggles to ask, to let someone in,
For vulnerability feels like admitting a sin,

And so, he carries the loneliness inside,
A companion he wishes he could set aside.

Yet even in the loneliness, a hope remains,
That one day someone will ease the pain,
Someone who listens, who stays through the night,
Who helps him believe it'll all be alright.

**Men also cry.**
For the loneliness they can't escape.

# The Weight of Expectations

From the moment he takes his first breath,
He's handed a script to follow till death,
"Be strong, be bold, provide, protect,"
A life dictated by what others expect.

He's told he must conquer, that failure's a crime,
To climb every mountain, to master his time,
He must never falter, never delay,
A constant race in society's relay.

But who asks him what he truly desires?
What ignites his heart, what fuels his fires?
Who gives him the space to simply exist,
To deviate from the rules and resist?

The weight of expectations presses him down,
Binds his dreams, leaves him to drown,
He feels like a prisoner in his own skin,
Yearning for freedom, a chance to begin.

He smiles through the pressure, laughs through the pain,
Pretending he's fine, though it drives him insane,
For admitting it's heavy, admitting he's weak,
Is something the world refuses to seek.

He carries the hopes of those around,
Their dreams, their fears, the futures they've found,

And while he holds it all, with a brave front,
Inside he wonders, "What about what I want?"

For men aren't machines, they're human too,
With dreams and fears and feelings askew,
And the weight they carry, though unseen,
Can crush the strongest, no matter how keen.

**Men also cry.**
For the expectations they are forced to bear.

# The Fear of Asking for Help

He stands on his own, as he's been taught,
To solve every problem, no matter how fraught,
For asking for help, they say, shows defeat,
A sign of weakness he strives to beat.

But deep inside, the storms still rage,
Battles untold, a war in a cage,
He longs for a hand, a shoulder, a friend,
To remind him it's okay to bend.

Yet he swallows his words, keeps them inside,
Afraid of the judgment, afraid of the pride,
What if they laugh? What if they scorn?
What if his struggles leave him forlorn?

The fear of rejection keeps him bound,
To fight his demons without a sound,
He builds his armor, hides his scars,
Pretending he's fine beneath the stars.

But there are moments he feels the strain,
When the weight is too much, the hurt too plain,
And still, he hesitates, he won't let it show,
The fear of asking doesn't let him grow.

For men are told to stand alone,
To bear their burdens, to be the stone,

But stones can crumble, and so can he,
Under the weight of what no one can see.

If only the world could understand,
That strength lies in reaching for a hand,
That asking for help isn't a crime,
It's bravery shown time after time.

**Men also cry.**
For the help they're too afraid to seek.

# The Silent Sacrifices

He gives up dreams he once held dear,
Trading ambition for duty, year after year,
The sacrifices he makes are quiet, unseen,
Yet they shape the life he's never been.

He lets go of the paths he wanted to take,
So others can thrive, for their sake,
He sets aside desires, ambitions, and goals,
Bearing the weight of familial roles.

No one asks what he left behind,
The pieces of self he can't rewind,
They see him provide, they see him endure,
But not the dreams he had to obscure.

He doesn't speak of what he's let go,
For fear it may seem like he wants them to know,
That even in giving, there's an ache in his chest,
A longing for the things he suppressed.

Every smile he offers, every step he takes,
Is built on the sacrifices he quietly makes,
His love unspoken, his pain concealed,
A life of devotion, his true self sealed.

Yet in the quiet moments, he wonders still,
If he'll ever have time for his heart to fulfill,

The dreams he put on a dusty shelf,
The parts of him he lost to himself.

But even as he mourns, he carries on,
For those he loves, he'll remain strong,
His silent sacrifices, his unspoken plight,
A testament to his enduring light.

**Men also cry.**
For the lives they've given up to build others'.

# The Burden of Protecting Others

He's expected to protect, to guard, to shield,
To face every danger, never to yield,
But in the depths of his heart, he feels the weight,
Of keeping everyone safe, of guarding their fate.

He stands at the front, always the first,
Shielding those he loves from every worst,
He takes on their fears, their worries, their pain,
While silently bearing his own strain.

The world expects him to be the hero, the knight,
To battle the darkness and bring the light,
But no one sees the toll it takes inside,
The cracks in his armor, the fear he can't hide.

For every time he holds back his tears,
For every sacrifice, for all his fears,
He wonders who will protect him in return,
When he's the one who's left to burn.

He hides his exhaustion, his doubts, his scars,
Hoping no one will notice the distant stars,
He's the one who must always stand tall,
Even when it feels like he's about to fall.

He fears that one day, he won't be enough,
That his strength will falter, the road will be tough,

That the weight of everyone's world on his back
Will break him down, and he'll lose track.

Yet still, he presses on, without a sound,
Because he's the one who's always around,
To protect, to guard, to keep them safe,
Even if he feels like he can't escape.

**Men also cry.**
For the burden of always being the protector.

# The Struggle with Identity

Who am I, when the world tells me who to be?
A man of strength, devoid of fragility.
They say I should be stoic, strong, and bold,
But inside, I'm a story yet untold.

I wear the mask that's expected of me,
I hide my doubts, so no one can see.
I'm told to be successful, to never fail,
But what happens when I question this tale?

Who am I beyond the roles I play?
The worker, the brother, the partner, the prey?
Where do I stand when I'm stripped of these names,
When the world's expectations start to feel like chains?

I'm more than the labels the world wants to assign,
More than the box that's drawn so fine,
But every time I try to break free,
I'm pulled back into what they want me to be.

I want to show my real self, my true core,
But I fear it will never be enough, no more.
Will they accept the man I am inside,
Or will they turn away, with nowhere to hide?

This struggle with identity, so deep and so raw,
Leaves me questioning the man I saw.

Am I who I want to be, or just who they say?
A reflection of their hopes, their dreams, their way.

For in the silence, I ask myself still,
Who am I truly? What do I feel?
Beyond the roles, beyond the mask,
What's left of me if I dare to ask?

**Men also cry.**
For the identity they can't fully express.

# The Fear of Showing Vulnerability

To be vulnerable is to be weak,
At least that's what the world says, so to speak.
But beneath the surface, the heart longs to show,
The emotions he hides, the feelings below.

He wants to cry, to let the tears fall,
To speak of his pain, to admit it all,
But he's been taught that men don't break,
That strength means never letting the heart ache.

The fear of being judged keeps him in line,
Afraid of showing the cracks that define,
What makes him human, what makes him real,
The things that he feels but can't reveal.

What if they see him as less than strong?
What if they tell him he's wrong, all along?
What if they laugh or turn away,
Unable to understand the price he pays?

So he keeps it in, builds up the walls,
Pretending he's fine, when the silence calls.
He forces a smile, hides his pain,
Fears that being open will drive him insane.

But deep inside, he knows the truth—
Vulnerability doesn't steal his youth,

It doesn't take away his might,
But shows him a deeper, truer light.

For being vulnerable is not a crime,
It's part of the strength that comes with time,
To show the world your fears and scars,
Is to own your story, to reach for the stars.

**Men also cry.**
For the vulnerability they're afraid to show.

# The Mask of Strength

He wears the mask of strength every day,
A shield of courage that hides the fray,
But behind the façade, he is broken inside,
Hiding the truth, the pain he can't confide.

He's taught to stand tall, to never bend,
To be unshaken, to never pretend,
But every smile, every firm hand,
Hides a man who struggles to understand.

The mask he wears is heavy and tight,
It keeps out the darkness but dims his light,
He feels like a stranger in his own skin,
Longing for someone to let him in.

Yet the world sees only what he shows,
A man of steel, with no room for woes,
So he keeps up the act, pretending to be whole,
While the cracks deepen, swallowing his soul.

What would happen if he let it slip,
If he dropped the mask and let it rip?
Would they still see him as strong, as true,
Or would they walk away, afraid of the view?

**Men also cry.**
For the mask of strength they feel forced to wear.

# The Fear of Judgment

He fears the judgment of others' eyes,
The whispers, the stares, the silent cries,
What if they see him as weak, as frail,
What if his vulnerability makes him fail?

It's easier to pretend, to hold it in,
To bury his feelings, to never begin,
To share the tears, to voice the ache,
For fear that it will be too much to take.

The weight of their opinions crushes his heart,
So he keeps his distance, stays apart,
Hiding the parts that are soft, that break,
Afraid of the judgment he cannot shake.

Yet inside, he wishes for someone to see,
To understand the pain that won't set him free,
He wants to be real, to let down his guard,
But the fear of rejection makes it hard.

What if they turn their backs, walk away,
When they learn the truth he's kept at bay?
So he holds on tight to the fear inside,
And continues to hide, to silently abide.

**Men also cry.**
For the fear of judgment that keeps them silent.

# The Burden of Perfection

Every day he strives to be enough,
To be perfect, to be tough,
To be the man they want him to be,
Never showing weakness, never setting free.

He's told that perfection is the goal,
That he must be flawless, whole,
But the pressure to succeed, to never fail,
Is a heavy burden, a constant travail.

He beats himself up when he's not enough,
When the world tells him he's too rough,
When the standards are too high to meet,
And perfection feels like a bitter defeat.

He wants to let go, to be just himself,
To stop chasing perfection, to place it on the shelf,
But the fear of falling short holds him tight,
Afraid that imperfection will dim his light.

He wonders if he's allowed to make mistakes,
To show the world that he, too, breaks,
But the fear of imperfection never lets him go,
And so he keeps up the charade, hiding the woe.

**Men also cry.**
For the burden of perfection they can't escape.

# The Fear of Being Vulnerable in Love

In love, he's told to be the strong one,
To protect, to cherish, to never run,
But the fear of vulnerability in love is deep,
A wound he hides, a secret to keep.

He fears that loving too much will break him down,
That showing his heart will make him drown,
What if she sees his flaws, his fears,
And decides to walk away from all those tears?

He wants to love freely, to be open and true,
But the fear of rejection holds him through,
For what if she doesn't accept the parts of him,
That are broken, scared, and dim?

He longs to show her the man inside,
But the vulnerability feels like he's denied,
The chance to be loved, to be whole,
Without hiding the cracks in his soul.

But love is not just about strength and might,
It's about being seen in the darkest night,
And though he fears it, he needs to believe,
That love isn't just about what he can achieve.

**Men also cry.**

For the vulnerability they're afraid to show in love.

# The Struggle to Open Up

He struggles with opening up, with speaking his mind,
For words are hard when they're tangled and blind,
He wants to share, to be heard, to be real,
But the vulnerability feels too surreal.

What if they don't understand what he's feeling?
What if they laugh or find it unappealing?
What if his words get lost in translation,
And he's left with a deeper isolation?

He's been taught to stay strong, to remain composed,
To keep his emotions neatly enclosed,
But inside, the thoughts swirl, the pain grows,
And he wonders if anyone truly knows.

The more he holds back, the heavier it gets,
The weight of emotions, the unspoken threats,
But opening up feels like exposing a wound,
One that he's tried to keep safely marooned.

Yet he knows that silence doesn't heal,
That holding it all in makes him less real,
And so he takes the leap, though it's hard,
And hopes that someone will hear the broken guard.

**Men also cry.**
For the struggle to open up and let it all out.

# The Fear of Losing Control

He's always expected to be the one in charge,
To steer the ship, to lead at large,
To have the answers, to never be lost,
No matter the storm, no matter the cost.

But inside, there's a constant fight,
The fear of losing control at night,
What if the weight becomes too great,
What if he falters, what if he's late?

He holds everything together, a perfect façade,
But deep down, the fear of losing it is raw,
What if he breaks under the pressure he feels,
What if he's unable to deal with the wheels?

He tries to stay steady, to keep his mind clear,
But every moment, the fear is near,
The fear of failing, of losing his ground,
Of having no answers, no voice, no sound.

He's afraid of the chaos that could erupt,
Of losing control and being corrupt,
For without control, who would he be?
What if he's not enough for all he must be?

But everyone depends on him to stay strong,
To keep it all together, to play along,

And so, he carries the weight, with no place to fall,
Fearing that one day, he'll lose it all.

**Men also cry.**
For the fear of losing control and failing.

# The Invisibility of His Pain

He's been taught to keep it inside,
To suffer alone, to never confide,
His pain is invisible, never seen,
Hidden behind a smile so serene.

The world doesn't notice the weight he bears,
The way he stumbles, the silent prayers,
He's told to be tough, to never complain,
But inside, he's wracked with silent pain.

He longs for someone to see his hurt,
To notice the scars beneath his shirt,
But no one asks, no one inquires,
About the fire that silently expires.

His pain doesn't matter, not in their eyes,
For men aren't supposed to cry, to empathize,
He's supposed to be strong, to push through the ache,
But the truth is, he's starting to break.

He's invisible in his suffering, hidden in the crowd,
Fighting battles no one knows about,
He wishes for someone to simply ask,
"Are you okay?" beyond the mask.

But he keeps it in, just like they've told,
His pain stays quiet, his story untold,

For it's easier to suffer alone, in silence,
Than to risk being vulnerable and defiant.

**Men also cry.**
For the invisibility of their pain.

# The Silence of Expectations

He wakes up each day with a list in mind,
Tasks to accomplish, duties assigned,
He's expected to meet them, to excel,
But no one asks how he feels or what he'll tell.

There's a silence in the air, an unspoken demand,
To perform, to produce, to always withstand,
He's never given a moment to rest,
Always pushing, always striving for the best.

But beneath the silence, there's a growing ache,
The pressure to be perfect, to never break,
To meet the standards, to play the part,
To keep up the pace, to give his heart.

No one hears the toll it takes,
The mental exhaustion, the sleepless wakes,
He's drowning in the silence of their hopes,
Climbing ladders, tied to their ropes.

He wishes for someone to understand,
The invisible weight, the unspoken demand,
But no one asks how he's holding up,
As he fills their cup, never enough.

The silence of expectations is loud and clear,
Yet no one knows the cost of the fear,

That one day, he'll burn out, lose his spark,
But for now, he keeps it inside, in the dark.

**Men also cry.**
For the silence of expectations.

# The Pain of Never Being Enough

He works hard, he gives it all,
To be the man they want, to stand tall,
But no matter how much he does or gives,
It feels like it's never enough to live.

The world tells him that he must achieve,
That success and wealth are what he must believe,
But what happens when he gives it his best,
And still feels like he's failing the rest?

He strives to be perfect, to meet every goal,
But it's never enough to satisfy his soul,
He wonders what more he must do to prove,
That he's worthy, that he's got the right groove.

He gives his time, his heart, his mind,
But it seems like the world is never kind,
To the man who's always striving to please,
Only to find himself on his knees.

The pain of never being enough is deep,
A wound he's learned to bury, to keep,
For no matter how hard he tries,
The bar keeps rising, the praise denies.

**Men also cry.**
For the pain of never being enough.

# The Struggle with Loneliness

In a crowd, he feels alone,
Surrounded by faces, but none of his own,
He smiles, he laughs, he fits the mold,
But inside, he's empty, feeling cold.

The pressure to always be strong,
To never show weakness, to belong,
Leaves him isolated, pushed aside,
Afraid to show the loneliness he hides.

He's told to be the one to stand tall,
To never ask for help, to give his all,
But when the day ends, and the noise dies down,
He's left with the silence, the endless frown.

No one sees the nights he spends awake,
Wondering what's real, what's at stake,
For even when he's surrounded by friends,
He feels like no one truly understands.

The loneliness creeps in, silent and slow,
A companion that never lets him go,
And he wonders if it's a part of his fate,
To always be alone, no matter how great.

**Men also cry.**
For the loneliness they can't shake.

# The Burden of Responsibility

He carries the weight of the world alone,
A heavy load, yet he's never shown,
The pressure to provide, to always succeed,
To fulfill the needs, to meet the creed.

Every day, he wakes with the thought,
Of all the responsibilities life has brought,
To care for his family, to support his peers,
To silence his own doubts and fears.

He's told to be the rock, the one who stands firm,
To never let the tide crash, to never squirm,
But inside, he's exhausted, running on fumes,
The burden of responsibility in his rooms.

No one asks if he's okay, if he's strong,
If he's carrying a load that's gone on too long,
He's always the one who picks up the slack,
The one who gives, never turning back.

But deep down, he wonders how long he can last,
Before the burden overwhelms him, too vast,
He longs for a moment to take a breath,
But the weight of responsibility brings him to death.

**Men also cry.**
For the burden of responsibility they silently bear.

# The Desire for Approval

He seeks approval from the ones he loves,
From the world, from the stars above,
For all his actions, for every step,
Hoping someone sees him, someone will accept.

It's not just for praise or for the fame,
But a quiet yearning to feel the same,
To be validated, to be seen,
For all the effort, all the things he's been.

He works so hard, yet it feels like a chase,
A constant battle to win their grace,
What if he's never enough for them to see,
The man he is, the person he's meant to be?

He's told to be confident, to never doubt,
But inside, he's wondering what it's all about,
Does anyone notice the heart behind his eyes,
The man who tries, who constantly complies?

He's tired of seeking approval that's never enough,
Hoping for recognition, but life is tough,
He wants to be seen for who he truly is,
Not just a man chasing validation, trying to fit.

**Men also cry.**
For the desire for approval they can't seem to gain.

# The Fear of Letting Go

Letting go feels like a dangerous act,
For everything he holds is a sacred pact,
His dreams, his goals, his expectations,
All the promises, all the foundations.

He's afraid that if he lets go,
Everything will fall, everything will show,
That beneath the surface, he's uncertain,
That his life's a fragile, fading curtain.

He holds on tight, with clenched fists,
To all that he's built, to the dreams he's missed,
For the fear of letting go is far too strong,
What if he's left with nothing, nothing to belong?

The past has a hold, the future unclear,
But still, he clings to what's near,
He's afraid of change, of what may come,
Of losing himself, of becoming numb.

But in his heart, he knows the truth,
That letting go is a step to renew,
To free himself from the chains he's made,
To face the unknown, and no longer be afraid.

**Men also cry.**

For the fear of letting go and losing control.

# The Hidden Desire for Companionship

He hides his longing, his quiet plea,
For someone to understand, someone to see,
That behind the stoic exterior, the silent man,
Lies a heart that desires to be held, to stand.

He wants companionship, someone to share,
The moments of joy, the moments of despair,
But he's afraid to ask, afraid to show,
That he, too, needs someone to let him grow.

The fear of rejection, the pain of being alone,
Keeps him distant, keeps him unknown,
He's always the one who gives, who cares,
But who will be there to ease his fears?

He wishes for someone to hear his heart,
To be the one to never depart,
To be his partner, his friend, his guide,
But he keeps it all hidden, locked inside.

The desire for companionship is soft, yet loud,
But he hides it beneath a silent shroud,
Afraid that wanting too much will push them away,
So he holds it in, day after day.

**Men also cry.**
For the hidden desire for companionship they cannot express.

# The Fear of Being Seen as Weak

He fears being seen as fragile or frail,
As someone who's broken, who's destined to fail,
The world tells him to be tough and resilient,
But inside, he feels anything but brilliant.

He's afraid of being seen as soft, as less,
For weakness is something he can't confess,
He must always be strong, always in control,
Hiding the cracks, suppressing his soul.

What if they look at him and see his tears?
What if they judge him, amplify his fears?
The thought of being seen as weak is unbearable,
To be vulnerable, to be transparent, to be shareable.

Yet he knows deep down that strength is not just a pose,
That weakness can be beautiful, a chance to grow,
But the fear of judgment, of losing his place,
Keeps him locked in this endless race.

He wishes he could let go of this fear,
To show the world what's really here,
But the fear of being seen as weak runs deep,
And so he hides, his emotions to keep.

**Men also cry.**
For the fear of being seen as weak and broken.

# The Need for Solitude

He craves solitude, a moment to breathe,
Away from the world, away from the need,
To always be on, to always perform,
To always be the rock, to weather the storm.

The world never asks him to take a break,
To pause, to rest, to take time for his sake,
He's expected to keep going, to keep on track,
Never faltering, never looking back.

But the need for solitude is deep within,
A craving for silence, a place to begin,
To process the thoughts, the emotions he hides,
To give himself permission to let go of the tides.

He's always surrounded, always in demand,
But in those moments of solitude, he takes a stand,
To connect with himself, to find his peace,
To let go of the chaos and simply release.

But even in solitude, he wonders if it's right,
To take time for himself, to give up the fight,
Yet in those quiet moments, he finds clarity,
A chance to reflect and be free of disparity.

**Men also cry.**
For the need for solitude they rarely get to find.

# The Burden of Unspoken Dreams

He has dreams that he hides away,
Ambitions he never dares to say,
The world tells him to follow the path,
But he wonders if it's the one he's meant to have.

He wants to be more than what they expect,
To break free from the mold, to disconnect,
But fear holds him back, the burden of doubt,
The fear that his dreams will turn out to be a rout.

He carries these dreams in silence, alone,
Afraid that they'll never be fully known,
For what if they're too big, too bold,
What if they're dreams that are never to be told?

The world tells him to play it safe,
To follow the rules, to keep the pace,
But inside, his dreams are calling loud,
Begging for the chance to stand proud.

But the burden of unspoken dreams weighs him down,
A silent anchor that keeps him from wearing the crown,
He wishes for the courage to speak them aloud,
To chase his dreams, to stand unbowed.

**Men also cry.**
For the burden of unspoken dreams they can never voice.

# The Silent Struggles of Fatherhood

Fatherhood is painted as strength and pride,
But there's a story beneath that men often hide.
The sleepless nights, the endless care,
The pressure to always be there.

He's expected to provide, to lead the way,
To teach his children and never sway.
But what of his doubts, his fears, his strife?
What of the sacrifices he makes for their life?

He holds their tiny hands and dreams big dreams,
But inside, his heart silently screams.
Am I enough? Am I doing it right?
Will I be the man they look to with delight?

He hides his worries, his uncertainties,
His longing for his own identity.
Fatherhood is a blessing, but also a test,
A journey where he gives his best.

Yet sometimes he wishes for someone to say,
"Your struggles are valid, it's okay to stray."
For he's more than just a figure, a guide—
He's a man with emotions he must confide.

**Men also cry.**
For the silent struggles they face in fatherhood.

# The Shadows of Past Mistakes

Every man carries a story untold,
Of mistakes that haunt, that silently scold.
The decisions made in moments of haste,
The regrets that linger, leaving a bitter taste.

He replays the past, a relentless reel,
Of things undone, of wounds that won't heal.
What if he'd chosen a different road?
Would his life be lighter, a lesser load?

But society tells him to forget, to move on,
To bury the pain, to act like it's gone.
Yet the shadows of his mistakes remain,
A silent burden, an invisible chain.

He wishes he could rewrite the pages,
Erase the guilt that silently rages.
But he knows the past is part of his tale,
A lesson learned, though it leaves him frail.

**Men also cry.**
For the shadows of mistakes they cannot escape.

# The Loneliness in a Crowd

Surrounded by faces, laughter, and cheer,
He feels a loneliness he cannot clear.
For even among friends, even in light,
There's a part of him lost in the night.

He laughs, he jokes, he plays his part,
But no one sees the ache in his heart.
The conversations feel shallow, the bonds feel thin,
As he searches for someone to let him in.

It's not that he's unloved or unappreciated,
But his deeper feelings remain understated.

Who can he trust with his darkest fears?
Who will see the man behind the veneer?

Loneliness in a crowd is a silent pain,
A longing for connection that's hard to explain.
He craves a bond that's raw and real,
A place where he can truly heal.

**Men also cry.**
For the loneliness they feel, even when surrounded.

# The Silent Yearning for Freedom

He's bound by roles, by duties, by ties,
By expectations that the world implies.
But deep within, there's a quiet plea,
A yearning for freedom, a chance to be free.

Freedom to explore, to chase his own dreams,
To break from the mold, to follow new streams.
Yet the weight of responsibility holds him back,
A pathless road, a narrowing track.

He wonders what life could have been,
If he'd followed the passions he'd once seen.
But guilt and duty keep him confined,
A caged bird with freedom only in mind.

Still, the yearning remains, a flame that won't die,
A dream of wings, of soaring sky.
But for now, he stays, grounded, contained,
Hoping that someday, freedom will be gained.

**Men also cry.**
For the silent yearning to live life on their terms.

# The Pain of Unspoken Apologies

There are words he wishes he could say,
Apologies left for another day.
To friends, to family, to loves once dear,
To those who've drifted, who are no longer near.

He replays the moments, the things he's done,
The hurt he's caused, the battles won.
Yet pride and fear keep his voice at bay,
Leaving apologies he can never convey.

What if he spoke? Would it heal the wound?
Or would it only reopen scars too soon?
The uncertainty silences his intent,
Leaving him with a heart that can't relent.

He longs for a chance to make things right,
To clear the shadows, to bring in light.
But unspoken apologies weigh like stone,
A reminder that some pain is borne alone.

**Men also cry.**
For the apologies they wish they could give.

# The Weight of Suppressed Dreams

He had dreams once, bright and vast,
But life's demands made them part of the past.
The artist, the writer, the traveler within,
All buried under the world's din.

He exchanged his dreams for a stable life,
For security, for his children, for his wife.
But sometimes he wonders, late at night,
What could have been, if he'd followed his light.

The canvas remains empty, the pages blank,
The roads untraveled, the ship never sank.
He tells himself it's too late to start,
But the dream still beats in his heart.

It's not regret, but a quiet ache,
For the chances he didn't take.
He hopes one day to revive the flame,
To honor the dreams that still whisper his name.

**Men also cry.**
For the dreams they suppress to fulfill their roles.

# The Unseen Struggle for Identity

Who is he, beyond the roles he plays?
A question that haunts his quiet days.
Is he more than a father, a worker, a son?
Or is his identity defined by what he's done?

He's told to be strong, to fit the mold,
To chase success, to gather gold.
But what of his passions, his soul's desire?
What of the things that set his heart on fire?

He struggles to find who he truly is,
Beyond the labels, beyond the abyss.
Is he allowed to redefine his name?
To step out of expectations and reclaim his flame?

But the world doesn't wait for men to explore,
Their identity often tied to their chore.
Still, he dreams of knowing his core,
Of finding himself, of being more.

Men also cry.
For the struggle to discover who they truly are.

# The Shadow of Identity

Who am I, beyond the mask?
A question men so seldom ask.
Defined by roles they've had to play,
Their own true selves fade far away.

A son, a brother, a worker, a friend,
But where does their own story begin or end?
Beneath the labels, a soul confined,
Yearns to be seen, to truly find.

The search for self is fraught with pain,
For freedom comes with heavy strain.
To break the mold, to dare, to be,
The man they've hidden, finally free.

**Men also cry.**
For the man within who waits in vain,
To rise above the worldly chain.

# The Pain of Being Misunderstood

He speaks in actions, not in words,
Hoping his love is felt, not heard.
But silence often builds a wall,
And leaves his heart misunderstood by all.

They say he's distant, cold, aloof,
But fail to see the deeper truth.
He loves in ways the world can't grasp,
Through steady hands and tasks unasked.

Yet, in his chest, frustration grows,
To bridge the gap, yet no one knows.
He aches for someone to truly see,
The heart behind his mystery.

**Men also cry.**
For the love they give that's brushed aside,
And the walls that keep their truths inside.

# The Quiet Loneliness of Success

He climbed the hill, he reached the peak,
But found no solace in the feat.
The cheers of crowds, the trophies gleam,
Felt hollow as a distant dream.

For in his quest to stand alone,
He lost the warmth of hearth and home.
Success, they said, was worth the price,
But left his soul as cold as ice.

He longs for arms to hold him tight,
For laughter echoing through the night.
To trade his throne for love instead,
To fill the void where dreams have fled.

**Men also cry.**
For the victories won, yet hearts that ache,
For the love they've lost, the steps they take.

# The Weight of Silent Dreams

He carries dreams that time forgot,
A painter's brush, a writer's plot.
The passions buried deep within,
Beneath the duties he's worn thin.

A boy who dreamed of stars and skies,
Now stares through windows with tired eyes.
The world called him to play his part,
But never asked what filled his heart.

Yet in the quiet, when no one sees,
He whispers dreams on bended knees.
Hoping someday, he'll find the chance,
To let his inner child dance.

**Men also cry.**
For dreams they've buried, hearts confined,
And paths they've left so far behind.

# The Fear of Emotional Intimacy

He longs to share his deepest fears,
To open up, to shed the years.
But trust, for him, is hard to find,
With scars that guard his heart and mind.

The world has taught him to withhold,
To keep emotions locked and cold.
But deep inside, he craves the light,
Of love that sees him through the night.

Yet every step feels like a leap,
A risk too great, a wound too deep.
He holds his words, his truths, his pain,
Afraid to lose, afraid to gain.

**Men also cry.**
For the love they seek, yet fear to show,
For the walls they build, afraid to grow.

# The Quiet Fight for Inner Peace

He walks through life, a storm inside,
A restless sea, a rising tide.
He battles demons none can see,
A war within, his destiny.

He smiles, he laughs, he carries on,
But peace, for him, feels lost and gone.
He yearns for stillness, for a calm,
A gentle breeze, a soothing balm.

To find himself in quiet lands,
Where nothing's asked, no one demands.
A place where he can simply be,
A man unchained, at last set free.

**Men also cry.**
For the peace they seek, the wars they wage,
And the dreams of rest as they turn the page.

# The Quiet Grief He Bears

He grieves in silence, without a tear,
For the losses he's faced, for the ones held dear.
The world expects him to carry on,
To shoulder the pain until it's gone.

But grief doesn't vanish; it doesn't fade,
It lingers in the heart, in the promises made.
The loved ones lost, the dreams that died,
He mourns them alone, with no one by his side.

There's no room for his sorrow in a world so fast,
Where men are taught to bury the past.
To move forward, to leave it behind,
To hide the ache that echoes in his mind.

He's expected to be the pillar, the stone,
But even the strongest can feel alone.
For in his grief, there's no outlet, no voice,
No space to cry, no comforting choice.

He remembers the moments, the laughter, the love,
The bonds unbroken, now stars above.
But the weight of the loss is too much to bear,
And yet, he tells no one; he doesn't dare.

The invisible grief becomes part of his soul,
A shadow he carries, never whole.

Yet in his silence, he still finds a way,
To honor the memories and face each day.

For grief doesn't mean weakness; it's proof of the heart,
A testament to love that refuses to part.
And though the world may not see his pain,
It lives within him, again and again.

**Men also cry.**
For the grief they carry in silence.

# The Tears That Time Conceals

Time moves on, they always say,
But for him, the pain doesn't drift away.
The memories linger, etched in his mind,
A piece of his soul, forever confined.

He aches for the voice he'll never hear,
For the hand once warm, now nowhere near.
The laughter that echoed, now just a sound,
Fading like whispers, never found.

The world sees him as steady, composed,
But within, a storm silently grows.
He carries the weight, unseen, unspoken,
His heart a mosaic of pieces broken.

No one asks if he's doing fine,
They see the mask, the perfect design.
Yet behind it lies a well of tears,
Built over time, through countless years.

For grief isn't fleeting; it doesn't expire,
It burns like embers, a quiet fire.
And while the world may forget the past,
He holds it tightly, making it last.

**Men also cry.**
For the wounds that time cannot erase,
For the love they miss, the empty space.

# The Echoes of What Was Lost

He hears the echoes in the night,
The faintest whispers of fading light.
A child's laughter, a lover's voice,
Moments lost beyond his choice.

Each echo tells a story untold,
Of memories cherished, hearts of gold.
He tries to hold them, to keep them near,
But they slip through time, disappear.

He wonders if they know he cares,
If they see the love his heart still bears.
For in his silence, he shouts their name,
Hoping they hear it, feel the same.

But the echoes fade, and he's left alone,
A man with grief that's all his own.
A weight he carries, a quiet cry,
For the lives that left, for the long goodbye.

**Men also cry.**
For the voices they'll never hear again,
For the love that lingers, unspoken pain.

# The Loneliness of Remembrance

He visits the places where memories dwell,
Each step a story, each silence a spell.
The park, the bench, the old café,
A life once vibrant now tucked away.

He walks through time, a ghost of the past,
Reliving moments that couldn't last.
The world rushes by, unaware,
Of the man who stands in quiet despair.

For in remembrance, he feels alive,
But also the pain of what didn't survive.
A paradox of joy and grief,
A bittersweet, fleeting relief.

Yet, he knows he cannot let go,
For these memories are all he'll ever know.
They're the fragments that make him whole,
The tether to his grieving soul.

**Men also cry.**
For the solitude of memories kept,
For the tears unshed, the love they've wept.

# The Guilt That Never Sleeps

He carries guilt like a hidden scar,
A shadow that follows him near and far.
For words unsaid, for deeds undone,
For battles lost he could have won.

He replays the moments, the choices made,
The painful truths that will not fade.
"If only I had tried," he thinks,
As his heavy heart slowly sinks.

The world sees strength, the man they admire,
But inside burns a quiet fire.
A longing to mend, to make things right,
To find some peace in the endless night.

But guilt is a thief, it never rests,
It clings to the heart, to the heaving chest.
And though he smiles, he cannot deny,
The pain of guilt that makes him cry.

**Men also cry.**
For the burdens they shoulder, the guilt they hide,
For the battles within, and the tears uncried.

# The Weight of Unseen Sacrifices

He gives without asking, without a sound,
His efforts unnoticed, rarely profound.
The things he does, the love he gives,
In silence, he hopes his spirit lives.

No applause, no cheers, no fanfare bright,
Just the quiet struggle in the dead of night.
For every sacrifice, every small deed,
Is a testament to his heart's quiet need.

The world expects him to give more,
Without questioning what's in store.
They never see the toll it takes,
The small pieces of him that slowly break.

His dreams fade, his wishes die,
But still, he gives, he doesn't ask why.
For in his heart, he believes it's right,
To sacrifice for love, without the light.

**Men also cry.**
For the sacrifices made in silence, unseen,
For the love they give, and the spaces in between.

# The Desire for Connection

He longs for connection, for someone to see,
The man behind the mask, who yearns to be free.
The world only knows the role he plays,
But inside, he hopes for brighter days.

To be understood, to be heard,
To find a soul who knows every word.
But in a world that moves so fast,
True connection feels like it's in the past.

He hides his longing, buries the need,
Afraid of rejection, afraid to plead.
Yet deep down, he craves to find,
A bond that heals, a peace of mind.

So he keeps it in, the loneliness grows,
A secret he wears, no one knows.
For the man who gives, who helps, who strives,
Is also the man who needs to feel alive.

**Men also cry.**
For the connections lost, for the bonds unmade,
For the love they long for, but feel afraid.

# The Fear of Vulnerability

He hides behind walls, behind closed doors,
Afraid to show what's at the core.
The world tells him to stand so tall,
To never bend, to never fall.

But inside, a storm brews with force,
A fear of being weak, of losing course.
To be vulnerable is a dangerous thing,
A place where the heart might break and sting.

He's taught to be strong, to never cry,
To keep his feelings bottled inside.
But the truth is buried beneath the shield,
A truth that he refuses to yield.

The fear of letting go, of losing control,
Keeps him locked in a tight, frozen hold.
But he knows deep down, in a quiet plea,
That to be vulnerable is to finally be free.

**Men also cry.**
For the fear of being broken, for the walls they build,
For the strength they fake, when their hearts are still.

# The Pressure of Perfection

He strives for perfection, day by day,
A goal he chases, come what may.
The world expects him to never fail,
To sail smoothly without a trail.

Every flaw, every slip, every mistake,
He carries it like a heavy weight.
The pressure to be flawless, to never fall,
Is the greatest burden of them all.

He works, he tries, he gives his best,
But inside, he wonders if he'll ever rest.
For perfection is a mountain too steep to climb,
Yet still, he climbs, time after time.

The world sees his success, his shining light,
But they don't see the tears at night.
For the man who strives for perfect grace,
Often feels like he's lost the race.

**Men also cry.**
For the pressure to be perfect, for the mistakes they hide,
For the fear of failure, and the tears they don't confide.

# The Struggle to Let Go

He holds onto the past with a steady grip,
Afraid to let go, afraid to slip.
The memories are all that remain,
A chain that binds, a silent pain.

He clings to the moments, the words once said,
Afraid of forgetting the love he's been fed.
But time moves on, as time will do,
And letting go feels like being untrue.

The people change, the faces fade,
But the heart still holds the love it made.
He knows it's time to move along,
But letting go feels so wrong.

In the silence, he feels the weight,
The struggle to leave, to change his fate.
For love is not something to simply discard,
And letting go leaves the heart scarred.

**Men also cry.**
For the things they can't let go,
For the love they lose, for the pain they know.

# The Battle Within

He wakes each day with the weight of the fight,
A silent war that consumes him at night.
On the outside, he seems to stand tall,
But within, he's afraid he might fall.

The conflict rages beneath the skin,
A struggle he fights, but rarely wins.
It's not a battle with others he fears,
But the demons inside, the internal tears.

He questions himself, his worth, his place,
Constantly chasing an impossible race.
In the mirror, he sees a man, but unsure,
Of who he truly is, or what he's meant for.

The battle is silent, with no loud cries,
No screams or shouts, no battle cries.
But inside, the war rages on,
A fight with himself that's never gone.

**Men also cry.**
For the wars they fight, and the battles they lose,
For the struggle within, that they can't refuse.

# The Burden of Expectations

He walks under the weight of what's expected,
A role he never asked for, but he's selected.
The world tells him who he must be,
A perfect image, so they can see.

He's told to be strong, to never bend,
To be a leader, a lover, a friend.
But no one asks how he feels inside,
The pressure he holds, the tears he hides.

He tries to meet every need, every call,
But the more he gives, the less he feels whole.
For the burden of expectations is a heavy crown,
A constant weight that drags him down.

He wishes for freedom, for release,
From the demands that never cease.
But he knows that in a world so loud,
It's hard to be real when you're lost in the crowd.

**Men also cry.**
For the burden they carry, for the role they play,
For the expectations that never fade away.

# The Silence of Self-Doubt

He walks in silence, with questions on his mind,
A voice within that's cruel and unkind.
Every decision, every move he makes,
Is weighed by doubt, for his own sake.

He wonders if he's enough, if he's right,
If his choices will lead him to the light.
But self-doubt whispers, a constant companion,
Reminding him of what he's lost, what he's abandoned.

He hides it well, puts on a mask,
Afraid to show the truth when asked.
The fear of failure, of not measuring up,
Is a poison that fills his empty cup.

Yet, deep inside, he yearns to find
A peace with himself, a still, clear mind.
But self-doubt lingers, a shadow so deep,
A reminder of promises he can't keep.

**Men also cry.**
For the doubts they carry, for the fear they wear,
For the silence within, and the burden they bear.

# The Weight of Responsibility

He stands as the pillar, the steady hand,
The one who carries, the one who understands.
The weight of responsibility, a burden so great,
He shoulders it alone, without debate.

Family, work, the dreams of the past,
All fall on his shoulders, held fast.
No one sees the toll it takes,
The exhaustion, the aches, the breaks.

He gives everything, without a thought,
Doing what's needed, without being sought.
But inside, he's breaking, piece by piece,
Wishing for a moment of sweet release.

He longs for someone to share the load,
To help him walk, to lighten the road.
But he keeps going, for there's no choice,
With each step forward, he silences his voice.

**Men also cry.**
For the weight they carry, for the load they bear,
For the dreams they chase, for the moments they share.

# The Fear of Being Forgotten

He works in silence, unnoticed, unseen,
A life lived quietly, behind the scene.
He wonders, in the quiet of night,
If his life will fade without a light.

The world moves on, leaving him behind,
His name lost in the sands of time.
He fears he'll be forgotten, erased from the past,
A fleeting moment that didn't last.

The people he loves, the things he's done,
Will they remember him when his time is done?
Or will he be a shadow, a distant face,
A forgotten figure in a forgotten place?

He tries to make his mark, to leave a sign,
But the fear of fading is his silent crime.
For in his heart, he wants to know,
That his life mattered, that it didn't go.

**Men also cry.**
For the fear of being forgotten, for the legacy they chase,
For the hope that they leave an enduring trace.

# The Invisible Man

He's always the one who shows up first,
The one to quench your deepest thirst,
A friend, a brother, a shoulder to lean,
But who's there when his soul's unseen?

He's the quiet force that holds it all,
The one you call when you start to fall,
With open arms and a listening ear,
But who will hear his voice when he's in fear?

He carries the weight without a sound,
A warrior who's always battle-bound,
But in the stillness, when the noise dies,
He's left to question, with tear-filled eyes.

His heart is full of all the love he gives,
Yet he wonders if that's how he lives,
Is it enough to be the one who cares,
When no one's there when he needs to share?

He walks through life with an invisible load,
Never asking for help, never showing his code.
For the man who's always strong, always true,
Is often the one with no one to turn to.

**Men also cry.**
But no one ever sees their tears,
No one hears their whispered fears.

# The Price of Selflessness

He gives with open hands, without regret,
But in his heart, there's an unspoken debt.
He's always there when others fall,
But who will catch him when he calls?

He sacrifices his time, his space, his mind,
To help others, to never leave them behind.
But deep inside, he wonders if it's enough,
If being selfless means living rough.

The love he gives, the care he shows,
Is never returned, or so it goes.
He waits for someone to return the favor,
But finds himself lost in his own behavior.

He gives and gives, yet feels the void,
The emptiness he can't avoid.
For the price of selflessness is high,
When the world takes, and he's left to cry.

**Men also cry.**
For the price of love, for the sacrifice they make,
For the things they give, and the hearts they break.

# The Mask of Resilience

He wears a mask of resilience, strong and true,
A shield he holds, never letting through.
The world sees him as unbreakable, unshaken,
But within, his heart is slowly taken.

He's the rock, the one who's always there,
The one who never shows despair.
But behind his eyes, behind his smile,
He's been running, for miles and miles.

He hides the cracks, he hides the pain,
He hides the storm that falls like rain.
For in his world, he's taught to stand,
To be a warrior, to take command.

But no one sees the weight he bears,
The battles fought, the endless prayers.
For the man who's always strong, always whole,
Is the one who's slowly losing control.

**Men also cry.**
For the resilience they wear like a crown,
For the moments they fall, and the times they drown.

# The Silent Burden

He carries burdens that no one knows,
Hidden beneath the surface, it grows.
The weight of expectations, of dreams unspoken,
A silent burden, never broken.

He doesn't ask for help, he doesn't complain,
He wears his troubles like an invisible chain.
For the man who holds the world on his back,
Is the one whose heart feels the lack.

He shoulders the pain, the doubts, the fears,
Without shedding a tear, without speaking the years.
But inside, his soul is slowly cracked,
For the burden he carries is never unpacked.

The world doesn't see, doesn't understand,
The invisible weight that's so unplanned.
But still, he carries it with pride,
Even as his tears subside.

**Men also cry.**
For the burdens they carry in silence each day,
For the weight they bear, and the price they pay.

# The Hidden Loneliness

He stands in a crowd, yet feels alone,
Surrounded by people, but no one's known.
The loneliness grows, though no one sees,
A quiet ache, a silent plea.

He's surrounded by voices, by laughter, by sound,
But inside, his heart feels unbound.
For the man who's always surrounded by cheer,
Is often the one who hides his fear.

He craves connection, a hand to hold,
Someone to listen, to break the cold.
But instead, he hides in the noise of the world,
Afraid to speak, afraid to be uncurled.

He gives his all, yet still feels this void,
A loneliness that can't be destroyed.
For in the crowd, he's still alone,
Longing for someone to call his own.

**Men also cry.**
For the loneliness they carry beneath the crowd,
For the silence they endure, and the pain unbowed.

# The Fear of Rejection

He puts himself out there, afraid of the fall,
Hoping his efforts will mean something at all.
He opens his heart, he shares his soul,
But the fear of rejection takes its toll.

He hides behind humor, behind a smile,
Afraid to show vulnerability, even for a while.
For every word, every gesture, every sign,
Is met with doubt, a fear so divine.

The fear that he's not good enough,
That his love, his friendship, is too rough.
He wonders if he's too much or too little,
A constant battle, a painful riddle.

Yet he continues to reach, to try, to care,
Even though the fear is always there.
He gives love, but in return, he waits,
Hoping that someone will open the gates.

**Men also cry.**
For the fear of rejection, for the heart they expose,
For the moments they hide and the truth they compose.

# The Need for Validation

He walks through life with a quiet plea,
To be seen, to be heard, to simply be free.
But deep inside, he longs for a sign,
A validation that he's worth the time.

He strives for success, he seeks the applause,
To feel like he matters, to feel like he's not lost.
But every step forward feels like a chase,
For something elusive, for a hollow embrace.

He works and works, but is it enough?
Will he ever reach the top when the world feels tough?
He seeks approval, from the world and himself,
A constant hunger, a thirst for help.

He's told to be confident, to never doubt,
But inside, he wonders what it's all about.
Will he ever feel whole, feel at peace?
Or is validation just a fleeting release?

**Men also cry.**
For the validation they seek but cannot find,
For the emptiness that lies deep in the mind.

# The Invisible Scars

He hides his scars beneath the skin,
Invisible wounds from where he's been.
The pain that no one ever sees,
The brokenness that never frees.

He's been hurt, he's been betrayed,
But no one notices the price he's paid.
He wears his pain with pride and grace,
Afraid to show it, afraid to face.

The invisible scars are etched so deep,
A reminder of the promises he couldn't keep.
He carries them quietly, without a sound,
Afraid to show the hurt that's always around.

For the man with invisible scars is strong,
He keeps going, even when it feels wrong.
But those scars, they don't fade with time,
They stay with him, a silent climb.

**Men also cry.**
For the invisible scars that they must hide,
For the pain they carry, and the tears they confide.

# The Fear of Being Vulnerable

He builds walls high, keeps the world outside,
Afraid to be seen, afraid to confide.
Vulnerability feels like a dangerous thing,
A weakness he's taught not to bring.

He fears that if he opens his heart,
He'll be judged, torn apart.
The world sees him as tough and unbreakable,
But inside, he's unsure, feeling unstable.

He longs to open up, to let someone in,
But the fear of judgment keeps him within.
What if they see him as fragile, as weak?
What if they leave him, afraid to speak?

Yet the more he hides, the more he aches,
The more he longs for real stakes.
For the man who guards his heart with care,
Is the one who fears the world will never be fair.

**Men also cry.**
For the fear of vulnerability, for the trust they withhold,
For the strength they fake, and the heart they fold.

# The Loneliness of Leadership

He stands at the front, leading the way,
The one people turn to, day after day.
But behind the scenes, when no one's around,
He wonders if he's truly found.

He bears the responsibility of the whole,
The weight of others' dreams on his soul.
But in the quiet, he feels the sting,
Of loneliness that leadership can bring.

No one asks him how he feels,
No one sees the wounds that never heal.
He's expected to be strong, to guide, to lead,
But who supports him when he's in need?

He's the one who lifts others up,
But who fills his empty cup?
The loneliness of leadership is a heavy cost,
A burden he bears, even if it's lost.

**Men also cry.**
For the loneliness of leadership, for the weight they bear,
For the silence that follows, and the weight of despair.

# The Struggle for Self-Worth

He stands in the mirror, questioning the face,
Wondering if he's enough, if he's found his place.
He seeks approval, yearns for praise,
But still feels lost, in a never-ending maze.

He compares himself to those around,
Searching for a way to be found.
Is he good enough? Is he worthy?
Does his existence have meaning, truly?

He feels invisible in a world so loud,
A man lost in the chaos, beneath the crowd.
He tries to prove his worth with every breath,
But his struggle continues, a battle with death.

The need for validation haunts him at night,
A struggle for self-worth, a constant fight.
But who will remind him that he's enough?
That he's worthy, even when life's rough.

**Men also cry.**
For the struggle of self-worth, for the fight inside,
For the worth they seek, but cannot find.

# The Fear of Being Unloved

He hides behind laughter, behind every smile,
Hoping someone will see him, if just for a while.
For in his heart, there's a deep-seated fear,
The fear that no one will ever come near.

He longs for affection, for love that's true,
But doubts always linger, always in view.
Does anyone really see him, beyond the facade?
Does anyone care for him, or is he just a mirage?

The fear of being unloved haunts him at night,
A shadow that dims even the brightest light.
He's told to be strong, to carry his load,
But inside, he wonders if he'll ever be loved, or if he'll
forever be alone on this road.

He gives and he gives, yet still, he fears,
That all his love will be drowned in tears.
He hopes for someone to understand his pain,
But feels that no one can truly relate to his strain.

And so he continues, a smile on his face,
Hiding the hurt, keeping up the chase.
But deep inside, the truth remains:
The fear of being unloved is a burden that stains.

**Men also cry.**
For the fear of being unloved, for the longing to be seen,

For the ache in their hearts, and the love they've never gleaned.

# The Heartache of Regret

He looks back at the choices he made,
The paths he walked, the price he paid.
Regret weighs heavy, an unshakable force,
A constant reminder of a different course.

He wonders how things would've been,
If he'd chosen differently, if he'd taken the win.
But the past is a shadow that can't be erased,
A haunting reminder of time misplaced.

The heartache of regret lingers on,
A wound that never truly dawns.
He questions every step, every turn,
Hoping for answers, hoping to learn.

But the truth is that regret can't undo,
The choices he made, the things he knew.
All he can do is live with the pain,
And try to move forward, despite the strain.

The heartache of regret is a bitter pill,
One that he swallows, against his will.
And though he may heal, the scar remains,
A constant reminder of his inner pains.

**Men also cry.**
For the heartache of regret, for the past they can't

change,
For the weight of decisions, and the feelings that range.

# The Burden of Unspoken Words

There are words left unsaid, buried deep inside,
Things he couldn't share, no matter how hard he tried.
The words he swallowed, the things he should've told,
But fear kept them locked in a chest of cold.

He carries them around, like a heavy stone,
The unspoken words, the thoughts unknown.
He wishes he could speak, to let it all out,
But the silence is louder, drowning him in doubt.

What if they don't understand? What if they leave?
What if his truth is too much to receive?
So he keeps it inside, locked away,
Afraid of the damage, afraid to betray.

But the burden of unspoken words weighs on him still,
A silent ache, a quiet thrill.
He wonders if anyone knows the truth he hides,
The emotions locked inside, like rising tides.

The words he never spoke are a silent scream,
A cry for help, a lost dream.
But he carries them alone, in his chest,
Hoping someday he'll find peace and rest.

**Men also cry.**
For the burden of unspoken words, for the silence they keep,

For the things they wish they could say, but never get to speak.

# The Pain of Unfulfilled Dreams

He dreams of a life he never reached,
Of the things he desired but never preached.
Unfulfilled dreams, like whispers in the air,
A reminder of the life he could've shared.

He wanted more, he wanted to fly,
But the weight of reality made him ask why.
Why didn't his dreams come true, why did they die?
Why did he let them go, without a try?

Unfulfilled dreams are a silent ache,
A longing that's deep, a constant break.
He wonders if they'll ever come alive,
If he'll ever get the chance to thrive.

But dreams left behind are hard to reclaim,
The scars remain, even when he plays the game.
He wishes for a second chance, a new start,
But the pain of unfulfilled dreams never departs.

**Men also cry.**
For the pain of unfulfilled dreams, for the life they couldn't find,
For the hopes they had, and the broken pieces they leave behind.

# The Unseen Battle of Self-Doubt

He stands before the mirror, eyes full of fear,
Afraid to face the reflection, afraid to be clear.
The world sees him as strong, as confident, bold,
But inside, he fights battles that remain untold.

Self-doubt whispers in the quiet of his mind,
Telling him he's not enough, that he's falling behind.
He questions his worth, his place in this world,
A constant war with the lies he's been told.

Why is it that no one can see the fight?
The hours he spends questioning if he's right.
The fear that he'll fail, that he'll never succeed,
That despite all his efforts, he won't be freed.

He hides his insecurities behind a smile,
Pretending to be fine, to walk every mile.
But deep within, he wonders if he's made for more,
Or if his fears will hold him back forevermore.

He doesn't share the weight of his doubt,
For fear that it will make him seem devout—
Devoted to failure, to defeat, to loss,
When all he's ever wanted is to pay the cost.

But through this battle, he learns to see,
That self-doubt doesn't define who he'll be.

It's the strength to rise despite the fall,
The quiet courage that lives in us all.

**Men also cry.**
For the unseen battle, the war inside,
For the quiet tears that they no longer hide.

# The Isolation of Success

He climbs higher, reaching the peak,
Chasing success, the dreams he seeks.
But the higher he goes, the lonelier it gets,
Surrounded by strangers, filled with regrets.

He wanted fame, he wanted to be known,
But the closer he gets, the more he's alone.
The applause sounds hollow, the cheers fade away,
As the distance between him and others begins to sway.

Success has a price that few can see,
A world full of people, but no one truly free.
He's lost in the shadows of what he's become,
A king on a throne, but no friends to welcome.

In the isolation of success, he wonders aloud,
Is this what it means to stand out from the crowd?
The world celebrates, but he feels no cheer,
For in his success, there's no one near.

**Men also cry.**
For the isolation of success, for the loneliness at the top,
For the empty victories, that never truly stop.

# The Ache of Unspoken Love

He loves her with a depth no words can define,
A love so pure, so endlessly fine.
But he never speaks it, never lets it show,
For fear that his love might never grow.

He watches her smile, he feels her laugh,
Yet he keeps his distance, walking the path.
Afraid that his love might be too much,
That it'll scare her away, or cause her to clutch.

He dreams of telling her, of holding her tight,
But the fear of rejection keeps him in the night.
The ache of love, unspoken, unshared,
A burden he carries, one he's never prepared.

What if she doesn't feel the same way?
What if his love only leads to dismay?
The uncertainty gnaws at him day by day,
But still, he stays silent, pushing it away.

He wonders if she knows, if she feels the pull,
If her heart is touched by the same quiet lull.
But he never says it, afraid of the risk,
And so, his love remains in the abyss.

The ache is real, the longing intense,
But he hides it all, building his defense.

And in this silence, he lives with regret,
For the love he'll never share, the love he'll never get.

**Men also cry.**
For the ache of unspoken love, for the hearts they keep,
For the love they bury, the secrets they weep.

# The Conflict of Self-Worth

He wonders if he's good enough,
If he's worthy of love, or if life's too tough.
The world tells him he must strive and prove,
That he's worthy of all he hopes to move.

But deep inside, he questions still,
Does he measure up to what others will?
Is his worth found in success or fame,
Or in the quiet moments, the ones that remain?

He searches for validation in others' eyes,
But finds that his worth can't be disguised.
It's a battle within, one he can't ignore,
The conflict of self-worth that settles the score.

He wishes for peace, for self-acceptance to flow,
But the conflict remains, like an unquenchable glow.
He's searching for something he can't define,
A truth about his worth, a peace to find.

**Men also cry.**
For the conflict of self-worth, for the struggle to believe,
For the endless quest to love themselves, to truly achieve.

# The Weight of Regretful Words

He speaks in haste, with words untamed,
Not thinking of the damage, not thinking of the blame.
The words escape, harsh and fast,
Leaving behind a trail that will forever last.

He wishes he could take them all back,
Undo the pain, cover the crack.
But words once spoken can't be erased,
And in their wake, hearts are displaced.

He regrets the anger, the hurt in his tone,
The things he said that should've stayed unknown.
The weight of regret hangs heavy on his mind,
For the words he spoke, now cruel and unkind.

He yearns to mend the bonds that broke,
To apologize for the words he spoke.
But the weight of regret lingers, tight,
And he wonders if the wound will ever heal right.

**Men also cry.**
For the weight of regretful words, for the pain they bring,
For the truth that silence often speaks more than anything.

# The Struggle for Balance

He balances his life on a tightrope, so thin,
Juggling his duties, the world's demands within.
Work, family, dreams, and desires,
He's constantly burning from multiple fires.

He wants to be everywhere, for everyone,
But finds it hard to juggle all that's been done.
He's pulled in a thousand directions each day,
Never stopping, never finding a way.

The struggle for balance weighs on his heart,
As he feels like he's falling apart.
He longs for a moment of peace and rest,
To find some balance, to do his best.

But in his efforts to keep everything in line,
He loses himself, his spirit declines.
He tries to be perfect, to meet every need,
But the struggle for balance is growing too steep.

**Men also cry.**
For the struggle for balance, for the weight of the task,
For the moments of peace that they can't unmask.

# The Quiet Strength of Letting Go

He holds on tight to the things he loves,
Fearing that letting go means falling from above.
The weight of his past, the ties that bind,
He carries them all, yet peace he can't find.

The world tells him to move forward, to let it be,
But the past lingers, like waves in the sea.
The people he's lost, the dreams that slipped away,
He's unsure of how to face another day.

Letting go feels like an impossible feat,
An act of surrender that feels incomplete.
How do you release what has shaped your soul?
How do you walk on, when you feel less whole?

But in the silence, he begins to see,
That letting go doesn't mean to cease to be.
It's not about forgetting or erasing the past,
But freeing the heart, allowing it to last.

For when you let go of the things that bind,
You make space for new dreams to find.
You release the hurt, the guilt, the pain,
And in that release, you break free from the chain.

Letting go is not weakness, but strength unknown,
A gift to yourself, a way to be grown.

It's the quiet power of peace within,
A chance to start fresh, to begin again.

And as he lets go, piece by piece,
He finds the courage, the strength, the release.
For in the quiet, he finally knows,
The power of letting go, and how it grows.

**Men also cry.**
For the strength in letting go, for the freedom to feel,
For the peace that comes when the heart begins to heal.

To everyone who has journeyed through these pages, thank you.

This book is more than words—it is a reflection of emotions, struggles, and truths often left unspoken. To the women who seek to understand the unseen, and to the men who carry these silent burdens, this is for you.

Thank you for opening your heart to these stories, for letting these words touch your soul. May this book inspire compassion, spark conversations, and remind us all that strength lies in vulnerability, and healing begins with understanding.

*The End*